NATIVE AMERICAN STORIES

FOR KIDS

12 Traditional Stories *from* Indigenous Tribes *across* North America

TOM PECORE WESO

Illustrations by
GLORIA FÉLIX

CALLISTO PUBLISHING

Published by Callisto Publishing LLC C/O Sourcebooks LLC
P.O. Box 4410, Naperville, Illinois 60567-4410
(630) 961-3900
callistopublishing.com

This product conforms to all applicable CPSC and CPSIA standards.

Source of Production: 1010 Printing Asia Limited, Kwun Tong, Hong Kong, China
Date of Production: September 2023
Run Number: 5034141

Printed and bound in China.
OGP 18

To my grandchildren, Curtis,
Frances, Natalie, and Aidan,
and also to my wife, Denise.

CONTENTS

INTRODUCTION

Posoh! Hello! *Posoh* means "hello" in my Menominee language. All young readers are invited to join me on this thrilling journey to visit 12 different Native American tribes. Together, we will read their stories. How did the world grow on Turtle's back? Why do rabbits live in **briar** patches? Where do people come from? Who invented corn? You will find some answers in these stories.

This book includes a story about the sun from my tribe, the Menominee Indian Tribe of Wisconsin. This tale I heard from my grandparents. We will read more stories set in all areas of the United States. The United States government recognizes more than 500 tribal nations. Each one is different. And each Native American nation has its own stories.

How the world came to be is one of the questions everyone asks: scientists, poets, and kids like you. You probably have many questions about the world. Stories are a way to answer these questions.

Animals often play a big part in the making of the first world. Native people understand that animals have much to teach us. We just need to stop and watch them. Many stories are about water, sun, and the earth, all of which are important to both animal life and human life.

Stories about flute music, songs, and the beautiful stars and moon are in this book. Love is also an important theme. A young man is lonely and wants to find a bride. How can he win her love? You can look through the stories to find some answers.

I hope you enjoy reading this collection. The stories may help you be thankful for your family's stories. Or you may finish this book and want to write your own stories. If you do, just take out paper and a pen and start writing, like I did.

The word for *hello* also means "goodbye" in my language, so *Posoh*!

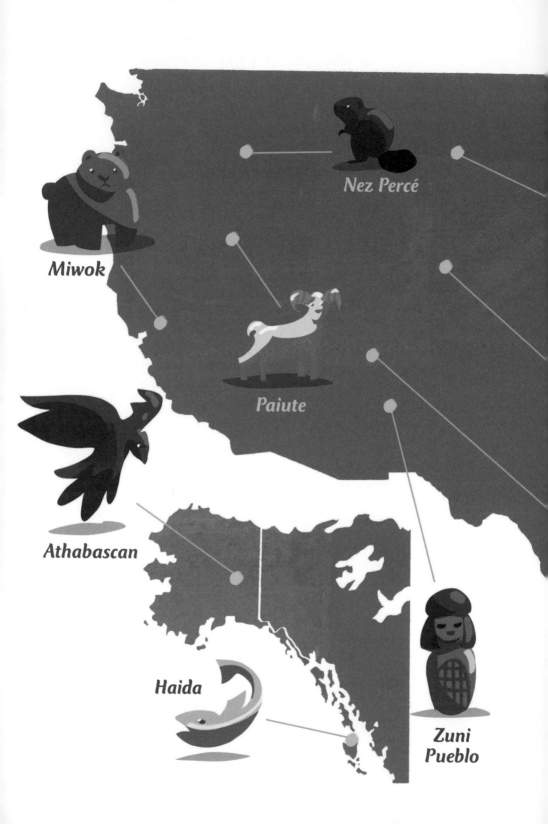

Nez Percé

Miwok

Paiute

Athabascan

Haida

Zuni
Pueblo

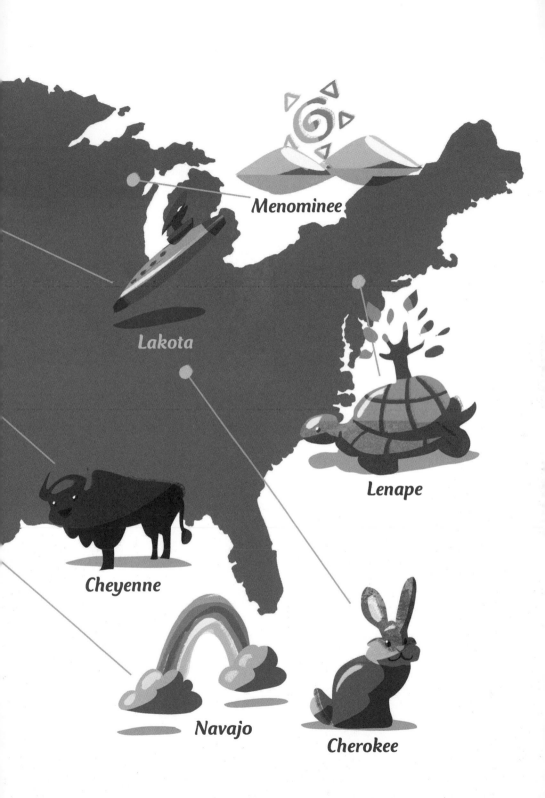

Menominee

Lakota

Lenape

Cheyenne

Navajo

Cherokee

THE WORLD OF ICE

Menominee

The Great Lakes Region

In the beginning, the world was made of ice. There were no towns, streets, or rivers. The only season was winter. No people lived in this frozen world.

One day a mighty spirit warrior named **Kesoq**, or Sun, woke from a long sleep. His body was made from fire because he was a star. He wondered if the rest of the universe was cold. He rose just a little and looked around. He saw only a great white blanket of snow and ice.

He wondered, "What lies below the ice?" He tried to walk, but he fell on the ice and hurt his knee. So Sun limped back to his warm home in the East and fell asleep.

When he woke, he remembered a dream about the white world. "What lies below the ice?" he wondered again. He rose higher in the East. He saw his tracks in the snow. Where he had stepped, the snow had melted. Wet, shiny rocks shone through Sun's melted footprints.

This time his **mukluks**, or boots, held him steady on the ice. He tried to walk. But still he slipped and fell on his bottom.

Sun said, "I am tired of this slippery-slide ice!" He went back to his warm home in the East, below the place of sunrise. He slept and dreamed for a long time.

When he woke, he went to the Great Mystery, the greatest power in existence, and asked, "Why is this outer world so cold?"

The Great Mystery answered, "Because the outer world has no sun."

Sun decided to return to the world a third time. He rose even higher, to the very top of the sky. He saw a big round lake of water where he had fallen. Everywhere he touched, his heat melted the ice. More gray rocks shone in the light. Pine trees grew from cracks in the rocks. They smelled wonderful.

Sun walked and walked. His heat melted more of the snow. Suddenly, the crash of cracking ice in the river sounded like thunder. His ears hurt from the noise. Sun ran back to his warm, quiet home in the East and fell asleep.

Sun woke after a long dream about a tall bear with white fur. He wondered if the bear was real.

Again, Sun rose in the East. He climbed all the way to the top of the world and looked north, south, east, and west. Floodwaters were gone. Cliffs rose along the river. Pine forests grew as far as he could see.

Sun searched everywhere for the white bear. Finally, he saw a bit of white fur flash from some rocks. He drew closer so he could see better.

Sun's heat melted ice around the tall bear covered in white fur. It came out of its rocky cave. Sun could see the bear's copper-colored tail. It was beautiful.

Sun decided to return every day to this new land. He wanted to see the great white bear with the copper tail that glows the color of fire. He wanted to see his reflection in the lakes and rivers. Kesoq the Sun Warrior returns every dawn to see his new world and everyone who lives in it.

The Menominee Indian Tribe of Wisconsin has lived in the lands between Lake Michigan and Lake Superior for at least 10,000 years. Menominee means "Wild Rice People." Wild rice is a grain that grows in shallow lakes and rivers. It is an important food because it is easy to store for use during winter. Both men and women are great hunters of bears, deer, elk, and moose. Menominee people mined **copper** ore for knives, cooking pots, and jewelry. They are also expert traders. They traded and sold wild rice, furs, and copper. This story tells how the sun is important in a snowy northern state. Today, about half the 9,000 enrolled Menominee people live in Wisconsin.

CHANGING WOMAN CREATES *THE* FOUR CLANS

Navajo (Diné)

Southwest Region

The Navajo or Diné people belong to their mother's **clan***. A clan is a group of extended family, both close and distant. Changing Woman created the first four clans. Here is her story.*

Before Changing Woman was born, First Man and First Woman lived in Dinétah, the Navajo homeland. It is in the Four Corners region of Colorado, New Mexico, Arizona, and Utah.

For many years First Man and First Woman were happy. Then they became lonely. First Man decided to climb Fir Mountain to pray for help. He sang as he climbed through dense clouds to the top.

Then a rainbow reached down from the sky. First Man heard a baby cry. He looked down and found a baby at the bottom of the rainbow. Her name was Changing Woman. He took this special baby home.

Many years passed. Changing Woman grew into a generous and good woman. She was old enough to marry, but no young men lived in Dinétah.

Sun rose every morning and shone on Changing Woman. Sun saw she was beautiful and kind. He turned himself into a spirit man. He was her husband for a short while, but the world needed his light and heat, so he returned to the sky.

"Will I ever see you again?" asked Changing Woman.

"Every evening at sunset, I will smile at you," he said.

After Sun left, Changing Woman had twin sons, Monster Slayer and Child Born of Water. The twins grew up to be heroes. They left home and became protectors of the earth.

Changing Woman was alone again. She wanted to see her husband, Sun. She followed the setting Sun west until she reached the Pacific Ocean. There she camped.

One day Changing Woman's sons came to visit her. "Hello, my sons," she said. "I have missed you. Tell me about your travels."

The two young men told her about monsters they had killed. They sat with her as Sun set. "Good night, Father," they said when the last light faded.

Monster Slayer and Child Born of Water noticed how cold their mother was. They built her a house by the ocean that could keep her warm.

"Thank you," she said to her sons. Then they returned to Dinétah.

Each evening Changing Woman talked to Sun. But he always disappeared into the ocean. She was lonely for someone to talk to during the day.

So Changing Woman created people from her own flesh. She took skin from her front, and it became the people of the He Walks Around One Clan. She took skin from her right arm. These people became the Towering House Clan. From her back she created the Bitter Water Clan. Last, she created the Mud Clan from her left arm. Everyone had to marry outside their mother's clan.

Soon many children were born. They wanted to return to Dinétah. Changing Woman gave them corn before they left. She gave them beautiful shells and stones. She taught them coming-of-age songs for girls when they changed into women. When Changing Woman heard the thankful prayers of the Diné people, she was no longer lonely.

When Diné people say their clan names, they remember how Changing Woman created them and gave them many gifts.

Navajo, or Diné, people are the largest nation in the United States, with more than 400,000 people. Many live in their homeland, or Dinétah, of Arizona, New Mexico, and parts of Utah and Colorado. Their language is similar to the Alaskan language spoken by their distant relatives, the Athabascans. Navajos are skilled **silversmiths**. They make beautiful rings, bracelets, and necklaces from **turquoise** and silver. Navajos learned to raise sheep from early Spanish settlers. **Mutton** stew is a favorite dish. Navajo women shear wool from the sheep and spin yarn for beautiful rugs. Their rugs show mountains, the sun, and spirit beings like Changing Woman.

YAHOO *AND* DENALI, *THE* GREAT ONE

Athabascan

Arctic/Subarctic Region

Athabascans live near the mountain peak of Denali in Alaska. It is the tallest mountain in North America. Once it was called Mount McKinley. Here is where their story begins.

Long ago in the time before people, a spirit named Yahoo lived in a flat land. He traveled the waters in a **canoe**. He tracked rabbits across snow in snowshoes. He sang fishing songs and hunting songs.

One spring day the snow melted. Moose mothers with their baby calves ate grass along the rivers. Salmon swam upstream to lay eggs. Yahoo was lonely when he saw all the animals with their families. He built a new canoe. It was big enough for two people. He would travel west to find a wife.

Yahoo paddled for one day. He made up a song for a new bride. He hummed his song but found no people. He paddled on. On the fourth day, he arrived near a village filled with large ravens. They lived in dwellings like people. He could see their fishing nets drying and could smell fish stew. He landed his canoe. He changed into his best shirt and combed his hair. Then he entered the village.

"Hello," he said to the Raven people. A group of Raven women greeted him. He sang, "I am Yahoo. I seek a beautiful and kind woman." He saw a lovely Raven woman hiding in the shadows. He repeated his song to her.

An older Raven woman came forward. "*Caw.* I am the wife of the Raven leader's second-in-command," she said. "My daughter is ready for marriage." She went to the young Raven woman in the shadows. They talked. Then the Raven leader's wife said, "*Caw, caw, caw, caw.* You may take my daughter as your wife." She led the young Raven woman to Yahoo. He took her warm hand. She had beautiful eyes.

The mother told them, "You must hurry. The first Raven Chief wants my daughter for his wife. He will kill you." Yahoo and his new wife ran to the canoe. They paddled away.

The Raven Chief blew a windy storm. Giant waves rose over Yahoo's canoe. Yahoo took a stone from his pocket and threw it ahead of them. He sang a magical song. The song calmed the waters in their path.

The Raven Chief threw his great spear at them. Yahoo saw the spear about to hit him and his wife. He turned a wave into a giant wall of stone. The spear bounced off the stone wall and broke. Yahoo and his new wife paddled harder. Sweat poured from their faces. They almost got away.

But Raven Chief blew harder. He created an even larger wave. He threw a larger spear. Yahoo heard the giant spear whistle as it neared him and his new wife. He raised his hand and turned the wave into an even larger wall of stone. The second spear hit the top of this huge stone wave and broke.

The angry Raven Chief paddled his canoe so fast that he could not stop. He fell head over tail and slammed into the earth. Then Raven Chief turned into an ordinary raven and flew away. Yahoo and his wife were safe.

Yahoo was tired from his journey. He fell asleep. When Yahoo woke, two new mountains had risen from the flat land. They were the two giant waves of stone. Yahoo named the larger one Denali, or the Great One. Yahoo made a song about the mountains. He sang it to his wife. She loved his songs, and she also loved him very much.

Athabascans are one of many groups of Native people in Alaska. They live along rivers and mountains. Some still hunt moose and caribou for meat. They trap beaver and rabbits. They fish for Salmon and whitefish in the rivers. At one time, they used toboggans, or large sleds, to travel in the winter. They wore snowshoes to walk in the snow. Today, they drive snowmobiles. In the summer they might use airplanes to travel to the nearest large town. Stories like this one help Athabascan children learn the trails to good hunting grounds. About 12,000 Athabascan people live in Alaska, and another 30,000 live in Canada. Athabascans speak a language similar to that of Navajos in the Southwest, but there are many variants, including 11 in Alaska.

TRICKY RABBIT *AND* *THE* TAR WOLF

Cherokee

Southeast Region

In the old-time days, the world was different. Animals were the people of the earth. There were Bear people, Wolf people, Rabbit people, Water Beetle people, and every other kind of animal people. Bear could make a loud growl just like today, and Wolf could howl a song with his family. It was a time of magic. The animal people could speak to one another.

One summer, everything changed. The sun shone all day and all night. It got very hot. Rivers stopped flowing. Lakes dried up. Worse, it stopped raining.

Drought was a new thing. The animals called a grand **council**. Yo-na the Bear asked, "What can we do?"

During this meeting, Tsi-s'dv-na the Crawfish proposed digging a well. Crawfish had strong front claws for digging. All the animal people agreed to share the work with Crawfish, except Tsi-s'du the Rabbit. Rabbit was lazy and **vain**. "Digging will make the fur on my paws too dirty," he said.

"Water goes only to those who help dig the well," said Bear. The animals dug the well for many hours. Soon their deep hole filled with water.

Rabbit watched the other animals drink their fill. "I'm thirsty, too," he said to Bear. Bear did not even look at him.

Rabbit decided to steal water. He snuck to the well each night and drank his fill. In three days, the animal people asked how Rabbit was able to stay alive without any water.

"I get up early and gather the morning dew," Rabbit said.

The animals did not believe him. "Rabbit is tricky," said Tsu-lv the Fox.

After Rabbit hopped away, Wa-ya the Wolf said, "No rabbit is smarter than a wolf. Let's make a trap by the well." The animals found a pool of sticky tar in the forest and formed it into a life-size model of a wolf. They placed the tar wolf near the well and went home.

Rabbit waited until all the lights in the animal village went out. "Perfect," he said. Rabbit came out of his house. He snuck to the well. He found the tar wolf in his way. He said, "Howdy, Wa-ya. Move over so I can have water."

Tar Wolf said nothing. Rabbit got angry. He kicked the wolf, but his foot got stuck. He kicked with the other foot. It got stuck! He kicked and kicked, but he was stuck.

In the morning, Wolf and Fox found Rabbit. They freed him. They called another animal council.

"How should we punish Rabbit?" asked Bear. "Let's cut off his tail!"

Rabbit laughed. "Do what you will," he said, "but please, don't throw me in that big briar patch."

"He fears the briar patch most," said Wolf. "Let's throw Rabbit into the briar patch!"

They threw Rabbit into a thorny thicket by the well. Rabbit ran under the thorny branches. He called back, "You can't hurt me! I love thorns! I love blackberries!"

The animals saw that Rabbit was a **trickster**. He behaved selfishly. He was vain. Ever since, Rabbit has lived by himself in briar patches.

Cherokee people once lived in Georgia, Alabama, and the surrounding states. Today, the Eastern Band of Cherokees is in North Carolina. The United Keetoowah Band of Cherokee Indians is in eastern Oklahoma. Cherokee Nation, also in Oklahoma, is the second largest Native nation in the United States. Cherokees were one of the first Native American peoples to have contact with Europeans and Africans. They shared corn, beans, and squash with the new settlers. They shared knowledge of how to build log cabins. They shared stories about the value of hard work and honesty, like this story about trickster Tsi-s'du. Many Cherokees speak the Cherokee language.

ZUNI ORIGIN OF CORN

Zuni Pueblo (A:shiwi)

Southwest Region

In the newly created world, according to Zuni **elders**, everything came from the five gifts of the creator: Father Sun, Mother Earth, Grandfather Water, Grandmother Fire, and corn. Zunis received corn as their last gift as they settled on the earth.

Zuni people began creation in dark worlds below the earth's surface. The journey from the underworld to a Place of Emergence on the earth's surface took a long time. During that time, the Zunis divided into Winter people and Summer people. Winter people included clans of Bear, Coyote, Deer, Turkey, Crane, and Grouse.

Summer people had clans of Sun, Frog, Turtle, Toad, First-Growing Grass, Tobacco, and Badger. Along the way, the migrating Zuni hunters learned to kill animals for meat. They learned many dances, prayers, and magical spells to bring hunters good luck. They saw some plants that were good to eat, but the land was dry. They learned how to bring rain.

One day as they were traveling, they saw a group of houses with fields around them in the distance. When they arrived, the Zuni leader said, "Hello. We are people from inside the earth."

The village leader replied, "We are the *A'-ta-a*, People of the Seed. We have power over seeds. We can plant seeds and harvest food."

The Zuni leader challenged them to a magic contest. "We can bring rain to make plants grow," he said. The Zunis danced and prayed to create a magical spell. For eight days, rain fell from the sky. The valley filled with rivers and lakes.

The Zuni leader said to the *A'-ta-a*, "See? This is our power."

The *A'-ta-a* leader said, "You are powerful, but we have a greater gift." He and his elders placed **prayer sticks** in the damp earth. For eight days they prayed and danced by the sticks. When they were finished, they invited the Zunis to see the results.

The Zunis saw a miracle. Seven tall corn plants grew from the earth. They had grown to full height in just eight days.

The *A'-ta-a* leader said, "These are our sisters, the Corn Maidens. They can feed you. The oldest is Yellow Corn of the North. She is the color of the winter's light." The Zunis admired her pale yellow beauty.

The *A'-ta-a* leader introduced the next younger sister, Blue Corn of the West. She was the color of the cold waters of the Pacific Ocean. The third sister was Red Corn of the South. She was the color of everlasting summer.

"Here is White Corn of the East," the *A'-ta-a* leader continued. Her flesh was as bright as early daylight. The fifth sister was Speckled Corn. Her flesh was multicolored like the morning and evening clouds. Then there was Black Corn, from inside the earth. Her flesh was as black as the caves.

"This is the last sister, the youngest," the *A'-ta-a* leader said. "We call her Sweet Corn. Her flesh is always soft." She smiled shyly.

The Zunis agreed that the *A'-ta-a* had powerful magic. The Corn Maidens could keep the Zunis from being hungry.

"Let's work together," the Zuni Seed Clan leader said to the *A'-ta-a* people. "The Zunis will provide water while the *A'-ta-a* will provide corn seeds to plant."

The *A'-ta-a* leader agreed if the Zunis would follow two rules. First, the Zunis must make prayer sticks when the Corn Maidens sing and dance. Second, no mortal person may try to know the Corn Maidens. The Zunis agreed. The *A'-ta-a* and the Zunis joined together to create a new clan: the Corn Clan. It exists to this day among people of the Zuni Pueblo.

The Zuni people know themselves as A:shiwi. They live on ancestral lands in northeast New Mexico in a settlement known as a pueblo. Their traditional homes were *adobe* rooms stacked on top of one another. The Southwest is home to 18 other Pueblo nations. Approximately 12,000 Zuni tribal members live on reservation lands, and some 80 percent speak their own Zuni language. Zuni people have strong beliefs. They hold religious festivals where they dance, pray, sing, and feast. Images from their stories, like the Corn Maidens, appear in their jewelry made of turquoise and silver. Zuni elders travel to the Grand Canyon regularly to the Place of Emergence from the earth's underworlds to pray.

THE HERO NAMED SWEET MEDICINE

Cheyenne

Great Plains Region

The Cheyenne hero Sweet Medicine began life as an orphan boy raised by his poor grandmother. Growing up in their small **prairie** village was not easy for him. His grandmother was not able to sew enough **moccasins** for him as he grew. His clothes had patches. He was often hungry.

As Sweet Medicine grew into a man, he became a skilled hunter. But most people did not know about his gifts because the old woman and Sweet Medicine lived at the edge of the village away from others. He killed his first buffalo and had a small feast.

That day a respected older leader came to their **lodge** and quarreled with Sweet Medicine. Even though the chief was wrong, he was an elder and his word was law. The orphan boy should not have argued with him. The Cheyenne peacekeepers chased Sweet Medicine away.

Sweet Medicine wandered aimlessly across the prairie for hours. In the distance, he heard voices. "Grandson, come this way," they called. Sweet Medicine followed the voices north through the grassland until he reached a **teepee**-shaped mountain called Bear Butte. This mountain is near Sturgis, South Dakota.

"Grandson, keep looking," the voices said. He found a cave and made his way inside the mountain. A tunnel opened into a large room. He was in a giant teepee filled with spirit people. He was frightened.

"Grandson, we have been expecting you," the voices said. "Sit down."

Sweet Medicine obeyed the spirits. They set before him a bundle wrapped in buffalo hide.

They opened it for him. Inside were four painted arrows. They were new and full of power.

"This is the great gift for your people," said the oldest spirit. "Two arrows are for war, and two arrows are for hunting." The arrows would remind Sweet Medicine of the laws for war and for hunting. He memorized everything the spirits told him so he would not forget.

"Thank you for these gifts," he said. The elder spirit continued, "Each arrow's power must be renewed each year. They will bring buffalo herds. They will protect you from enemies." Sweet Medicine listened and memorized songs, dances, and prayers that would help his people. He learned songs to bring buffalo nearby for hunters. He learned ceremonies for the Sacred Arrow Bundle.

After receiving a blessing from the spirits and a cleansing from sweet grass smoke, he returned to his home.

As Sweet Medicine approached his village, he saw starving children. He fed the children from his supply of food. He gave them dried buffalo meat to take to their parents. Then he entered the village.

Everyone was happy to see him return with food, for the buffalo had disappeared when he left.

Sweet Medicine set up a teepee in the center of the village. He purified it with sage smoke and sweet grass smoke. He invited people to enter the teepee with him. He taught them how to live correctly so the buffalo would stay and not go into hiding. He showed everyone the sacred arrow bundle and told its story. At dawn, Sweet Medicine sang the last sacred song for the ceremony to be complete. Everyone came out of the teepee and saw that the prairie was alive with buffalo. They hunted and had plenty to eat.

Sweet Medicine stayed with his people until he was a very old man. The Cheyenne people still have the sacred arrow bundle, and to this day they care for it.

The Cheyenne people originally lived around the Great Lakes. They are related to the Ojibwa, Cree, and Menominee people and speak an Algonquin language The Cheyennes avoided conflict with European settlers by moving west until they arrived in the Dakotas and Montana in the late 1700s. There they acquired horses. Buffalo became a main food supply, and they used the skins to make teepees. The Cheyenne people split into Northern and Southern tribes in the 1800s. Today, the Northern Cheyenne Nation, with more than 10,000 members, is in Montana. The Southern Cheyennes are federally recognized in Oklahoma as the Cheyenne and Arapaho tribes, with more than 12,000 members.

WHY *THE* NORTH STAR STANDS STILL

Paiute elders have a story they tell their grandchildren that explains the stars. According to them, Stars, or Sky People, are restless and travel great distances. They sometimes leave trails in the sky. But some Sky People do not move. One is Na-Gah, the Mountain Sheep.

When the world was young, Na-Gah's father was proud of his son. He gave the boy large earrings that looked like looped horns. Na-Gah wanted his dad to be proud of him, so the sure-footed boy decided to climb all the local hills. He kept searching for higher peaks. Climbing was how he sought his dad's approval.

Na-Gah was happiest when he was grazing in the highest peaks where his father could see him from great distances. He could climb higher than other young Mountain Sheep.

One day Na-Gah saw a peak higher than the clouds. He knew he must climb it to make his father proud. He circled the peak to find a crack big enough for him to get a foothold. But the peak was smooth on all sides. He could not climb up.

"Oh no, I am beaten," he said. "My father will be disappointed in me." He circled around the peak again and saw a hole in the ground. "Ha! I'll go into that cave and find a tunnel that leads up to the peak's top." He could hear his father call for him in the distance, but Na-Gah continued on.

The cave did lead upward. It soon got very dark. Na-Gah kept climbing in the dark. His father's voice grew faint and then disappeared.

Crash! Na-Gah slipped on some rocks. They tumbled down and sealed up the cave entrance below him. He was trapped. He had no choice but to keep climbing.

Na-Gah had never been so scared. He felt sticky spiderwebs all around him. He felt the earrings on his ears and thought of his father. Na-Gah did not want to disappoint him. He kept climbing up and up.

At last, Na-Gah saw a tiny light. "This could be the end of the tunnel," he thought. It was still a long climb, but now he had a goal. The light grew stronger so the climb was less scary. He finally reached an opening. He could barely squeeze his body through the hole. His eyes blinked in the sunlight. He looked around. He was on top of the highest peak in the world. "Father!" he called, but there was no answer. The walls of the peak were steep. He was not going to be able to climb down. The cave shaft was filled with rocks. Na-Gah was stuck.

Na-Gah found a small meadow with grass. He found water pooled in the rocks. He could look down on the earth from his perch. He would spend the rest of his days here.

About this time his father was searching for him among the Sky places. Na-Gah called to him, "I'm up here!" His father saw him. He grieved. He knew his son must spend his life on the peak.

"Goodbye," his father said. Then he turned Na-Gah into a star so everyone could see him. "Now you can set the north direction for all people," he said. To this day, Na-Gah is the North Star.

Stars shine brightly in the regions where the Paiutes live today: Arizona, Nevada, California, Utah, Idaho, and Oregon. In their language, *Paiute* means "traveler." Paiutes were nomads who traveled long distances to hunt, fish, and gather foods from plants and trees. They were made up of two or three main groups, and today about 20 independent Paiute groups are federally recognized. They have great knowledge of how to survive in dry country with few food sources. They have a rich tradition of stories, which may be told only in the winter, when animals hibernate. There are about 17,000 people of Paiute descent living in the United States today.

HOW BEAVER STOLE FIRE *FROM THE* PINES

Nez Percé (Nimíipuu)

Plateau Region

Before there were any people living on the earth, all the living plants and animals could speak and understand one another. Most cooperated, except the evergreen trees along the Grande Ronde River that ran through Oregon to Washington and Idaho.

The Pines and **Cedars** around this river knew the secret of fire. No matter how cold it got, the evergreen trees were able to stay warm. They would not, however, share their secret with others. Other creatures barely made it through each winter.

During the coldest winter ever, everyone was freezing except for the Pines and Cedars. Beaver's pond froze, so the beaver families could not leave their domed lodges. Willows by the river froze solid. **Birches** shivered.

"My family is freezing," said Beaver. "We will starve to death if we cannot leave our lodge."

"I am one of the last of my kind," said Willow Tree.

"Me-ee-ee too," shivered Birch Tree. All the animals and plants were at risk of dying, except the selfish Pines and their friends the Cedars.

Beaver learned the Pines would be holding a council near the Grande Ronde River. He had an idea. "I am lumpy and brown like the riverbank," he told a nearby clump of Willows. "I can hide in the mud and keep out of sight. I can take their fire." The Willows swayed in approval.

Beaver sneaked toward the Pines' bonfire. He watched the Pines bathe in the river. Then they sat around the bonfire to warm themselves. They talked and told stories.

Beaver lay against the riverbank. His big flat tail was frozen, and his toes had frostbite. He was about to give up when a coal rolled down the bank into his hands. He held the precious coal to his chest and ran. But as clumsy Beaver stumbled down the riverside, he knocked over rocks and made noise.

"Catch the fire thief!" yelled the nearest Pine. Beaver ran as fast as he could.

"Get him," yelled the other Pines.

Beaver ran in a **zigzag** pattern into the river. He looked behind him. Most Pines gave up the chase at the riverbank. Pine trees still grow in a thick bunch at that spot.

A few Pines led by an old Cedar kept the chase alive. "Stop, thief!" the Cedar called.

But Beaver was a strong swimmer. "You can't catch me!" he called. He swam into the deep part of the river. Cedar climbed a big hill to see where Beaver was going. He watched as the Grand Ronde River flowed into the Snake River. Beaver tucked the coal into his leathery paw and swam away into the distance.

When he got home to his pond, Beaver thawed his lodge and warmed his family with the coal. He gave a piece of coal and the secret of fire to Willows by his lodge. Then he swam downriver to give fire to a stand of Birch trees.

Since then, anybody who needs fire can take sticks of Willow or Birch. They hold the secret of fire inside them. All it takes to release fire is to rub two sticks together until they smoke.

For thousands of years, the Nez Percé, or Nimíipuu ("the People" in their language), have lived on the Columbia River Plateau of eastern Washington and Oregon stretching into Idaho. Today, their main land base is around Lapwai, Idaho. Nez Percé people developed the Appaloosa horse breed, which is known for its large spots. The Nez Percé were hunters and also depended on fishing to get them through the harsh winters. Today, fish are important for food and revenue. The Nez Percé Nation runs a tribal hatchery on the Clearwater River. The total population of the Nez Percé people is about 3,500 tribal members.

A YOUNG HERO FIGHTS *A* GRIZZLY BEAR

Miwok (Southern Sierra)

California Region

Long ago, Yosemite Valley in Northern California was known to the people living there as Ah-Wah-Nee, or Deep Grass Valley. It was the home of many bears.

One fine spring day, the leader of the Miwok people went fishing at a nearby lake. To get there he followed a trail that passed between boulders and trees, up and down through twists and turns. He looked forward to catching fresh trout for his family's dinner.

He was thinking of sweet trout meat as he followed the trail. He did not notice the giant female grizzly bear approaching from the other direction.

The huge brown bear, also intent on following the trail to the lake to fish, did not notice the human. She was grouchy from her long winter sleep. All she could think about was a big trout meal.

Much to their surprise, they bumped into each other.

"Hey!" yelled the man.

"Grrr!" growled the bear.

In the briefest moment, both recovered. Each thought about turning tail and running away.

But the grizzly bear would not retreat because she was so hungry and could not think straight. Besides, grizzly bears do not run from danger.

The man would not retreat because he had a proud heart. People of Ah-Wah-Nee did not run from danger, either. The two great warriors stared each other in the eye.

The man grabbed a big oak limb to use as a club. He raised it high, and *smack*! The oak branch landed on the bear's head. The bear swatted the man's head in return and scraped off some skin with her claws.

The man reeled back. He gripped the branch. *Whack!* The oak branch landed once more. "Take that," he yelled.

"Grrr," the bear replied. She swatted him again. Back and forth they went. The fight lasted for hours.

Toward the end, the bear was clearly winning. For every bump on her head, she left deep scratches in return. The man knew he was almost done. The bear stopped a moment and smiled.

At that moment, the man raised his club as high as he could and thumped the bear's head with all his might. *Crack!* The sound was like thunder. The branch split in half.

The bear stood tall and still for a moment. Her large brown eyes showed astonishment. Then she slowly fell flat on her face.

The man was exhausted. But he knew enough to crawl several feet away where he would be safe. Sometimes a grizzly bear will play dead. He waited several minutes to make sure the bear really was dead. When satisfied, he took out his knife and skinned the big bear.

He dragged the huge bearskin home. Everyone was impressed. Several younger men followed the trail to where the bear still lay. They butchered the bear and carried home the rich meat. There was more than enough meat to feed the entire village. They invited their neighbors for a feast.

People marveled at how brave this man was. They began to call him Yo-Semitee, which means "Grizzly Bear." After many years, his children and followers also began to be called Yo-Semitee. They remembered this story about their leader's courage.

People speaking a Miwok language live in four Northern California regions. Some live in the Sierra Nevada Mountains and meadows, like Yo-Semitee. Others live around Clear Lake in Lake County. Two groups live on the Pacific Coast. Today, the federal government recognizes 11 Miwok groups. They number about 4,000. They hunted in the mountains. Along the bays and coastlines, they collected mussels and fished. They also developed black oak plantings so they could harvest acorns for mush and flour. They played a game similar to soccer, with goalposts and an elk-hide ball. Many still hunt, fish, and play games in this region today.

SALMON BOY

Haida

Northwest Coast Region

Many years before today, an impolite Haida boy lived in Alaska on the Pacific Coast. "Son," his mother said, "you are no longer a baby. You must help catch Salmon." He kept whistling as she talked. "Quiet," she said. "You must help your father."

"Sure, sure," he said. His younger friends were playing at the river. He did not want to help with fishing.

"Come here," she said. "This is your first day fishing." She pulled out a shining new copper necklace. "This is for you, now that you are more grown up."

"Thank you, Mother," he said. He put the necklace around his neck.

When he left the house, he hid in the cedars, but his father found him and walked him to the canoe. "Sit here," his father said. "Watch."

The father and son paddled the canoe to a place where Salmon gathered. They set their nets.

"The sun is too hot," the boy complained. His father looked at him sternly, so the boy said nothing more. When it came time to pull the nets in, dozens of squirming Salmon filled the bottom of the canoe.

"They are so wriggly," the boy said. "I bet I can balance on them." He skipped across their bodies.

"Stop that!" his father called. "You aren't supposed to step on them! They won't let us catch them if we don't respect them."

That night his mother fixed a big dinner of Salmon, blueberries, and parsnip greens. "My Salmon is stinky!" the boy complained. He spit it out.

"Don't do that!" his mother yelled. She warned him that the spirits of the Salmon would get angry.

After the long lecture, he said, "I am sorry, Mother. May I go play now?"

"Yes," she said. "But be sure to take the Salmon bones and fins to the river and throw them back into the water."

"Why do I have to?" the boy asked.

"They will go back to the Salmon people and turn back into fish," his mother explained.

The boy took the basket of bones and fins with him. He was tired of all the rules about Salmon. In the distance he could hear his friends at play, and he was anxious to join them. He dumped the Salmon leftovers under a bush and ran off.

The boy went swimming with other children in the river. He was a good swimmer and swam past everyone else. But a current of water held him down. He drowned.

The boy looked around him underwater. There were many Salmon at the bottom of the river. They took him home to their village. He stayed with them all winter. They called him Salmon Boy.

The next spring, Salmon Boy and the Salmon all swam up the river. The Haida people were ready. It was fishing season.

Salmon Boy felt himself lifted into a net. "Oh, look!" a woman cried. It was his mother. She showed his copper necklace to her husband. "It is our son!"

She talked to him. Slowly, he remembered human words. After eight days, his fish scales fell off. He was human again. "Mother, I was wrong," he said. "I learned how to be a healer from the Salmon. Let me teach you their healing ways." He was respectful to her and his father.

Salmon Boy stayed with his family until he had taught them everything he had learned. Then he returned to the Salmon people.

Haida people live along the coast of the Pacific Northwest. They have communities in both Canada and the United States. In the United States, they partner with the Tlingit people in the Central Council Tlingit Haida Indian Tribes of the Alaskan government. Ancestors of today's Haida people have lived in the same area since the Ice Age. They carve large boats from cedar trees that could travel in the ocean. These canoes can hold 60 people. They lived by hunting, fishing, collecting shellfish, and raiding other tribal nations. When they celebrate important events, they might have a giveaway known as a **potlach**. It is a big feast where the host family gives away blankets, food, and other gifts. They carve totem poles that honor their family crests. Today, about 5,000 Haida people live on or near their traditional lands.

ORIGIN *OF* *THE* FLUTE

Lakota

Great Plains Region

Long ago, when the Lakota people lived in forests, not grasslands, a young man fell in love with a beautiful young woman in his camp. He was too shy to speak to her. He often went hunting to keep from thinking of her.

One winter day, meat was very scarce in the village. The man strung his bow and made new arrows for a hunting trip. The next morning, as the man was leaving, he saw the beautiful young woman at the river. "Goodbye," he whispered, but she did not seem to hear him.

Soon after he entered the forest, the man spotted elk tracks. An elk would give his family meat for many days. He followed the elk deep into the forest, but it stayed ahead of him. The man wandered off the trail as he chased the elk. By dark he was lost.

The young man set up a quick camp by a stream. He had a bag of dried meat pounded with berries and fat, so he ate this small meal. He sat against a tree and wrapped himself in his fur blanket. There he tried to sleep.

Owls hooted. Tree branches rubbed against one another. But no moon shone in the sky. The dark forest seemed alive with sounds, but the man could see nothing in the black night. Then he heard an **eerie**, beautiful sound. He fell asleep listening to it.

The young man dreamed of a redheaded woodpecker. It sang the same beautiful song.

When the man woke, the sun was shining brightly. He saw a redheaded woodpecker, just like in his dream. "Good morning!" it said. "Follow me."

"I dreamed about you," said the man. "I will follow you."

The bird flitted through the trees slowly. Its red feathers were easy to follow. The bird finally landed on the branch of an old cedar tree. The woodpecker hammered a dead branch until a hole was formed. Just then, a gust of northern wind arose and blew through the hole. The wind made a beautiful song in the hollow wood.

"Friend," the young man said, "may I have that branch?"

"Of course," said the woodpecker.

The young man found his way home with his cedar branch drilled by the woodpecker. He could not, however, make it sing. He prepared himself to pray and went to the top of a hill. For four days he **fasted** and prayed. During the fourth night, the redheaded woodpecker appeared. "Watch," he said to the man. The bird gave him directions for making a cedar flute.

In the morning, the man found a cedar tree and offered it **tobacco** before cutting a branch. Tobacco is a plant that can carry prayers from people to the Creator. He prepared the flute just as the woodpecker had told him. He carved it into the shape of a bird and colored the bird's head with red paint.

The young man took a deep breath. He made the flute sing a beautiful love song. It drifted all the way back to the camp, where the young woman heard it. When he returned to the village, everyone wanted to hear him play the cedar flute. The young woman looked at him and smiled. The young man played the most beautiful song anyone had heard.

Lakotas and Dakotas speak a similar type of Siouan language. People speaking these languages have lived in Minnesota, Nebraska, North Dakota, and South Dakota. Lakotas were known as horse experts and buffalo hunters. Men with war honors, as well as some women, wore eagle-feather headdresses. Sitting Bull and Crazy Horse are two of the most famous Lakotas in history. Joseph Marshall III, a Lakota author, has written numerous books about Lakota life. Lakotas have kept many of their traditions, including the seven values of praying, respect, compassion, honesty, generosity, humility, and wisdom. Some 115,000 people are enrolled in one of the seven Lakota tribal groups.

THE DELAWARE (LENAPE) CREATION STORY

Delaware (Lenape)

Northeast Region

Long ago, before the very first sunrise, there was nothing but empty space in all directions. The only living being was the spirit of creation named Kishelamàkânk, or Creator. During this long, quiet night, Creator fell asleep and began to dream of a warm yellow star rising in a blue sky. Feathered beings, birds, flew in the sky.

Creator liked this dream. The creation spirit kept dreaming and saw a place below the sky called Earth. Creator dreamed of moose, elk, deer, and rabbits. These animals grazed in fields of green grass and forests of tall trees. Flowers bloomed, and in fields grew corn, beans, and squash. Creator stayed asleep and dreamed of lakes, rivers, and oceans filled with fish, eels, turtles, and beavers. It was a beautiful **vision**, but, like all dreams, it ended. Creator woke up and looked around.

Now the space seemed lonely. Creator fell asleep again and dreamed of people. They were beings who could think. They sang, prayed, and danced. Creator stayed asleep for a long time, but finally came the time to wake up.

"That dream was wonderful!" Creator said. The creation spirit spoke words to describe the dream: "Sky, stars, sun, moon, Earth, mountains, and valleys."

As the words left Creator's mouth, the sky filled with stars, sun, and moon. The earth rippled into mountains and valleys. "Anything I say comes alive," Creator thought. "I must be careful with words." Creator continued to speak. "Birds, elk, deer, moose, fish, eels, beavers, turtles, frogs," Creator said, "I must create a world full of all these beings."

Creation was a big job, so Creator had a vision of the four Keepers of Creation. The creation spirit said, "Keepers of Creation," and they came into existence.

The Keepers circled around the Creator. The first was the Grandfather of the North. He gives physical form to the Creator's visions through rocks and the land. He also controls the winter.

The second spirit being was the Grandfather of the East. He controls the wind and is responsible for Lenape knowledge and creativity. Spring is his season.

The third spirit being was Grandmother of the South. She has the power of fire. Without her, all living beings would freeze to death. She controls summer.

The fourth and last Keeper was Grandfather of the West. His power is to bring rain. All living beings need water for life. He controls autumn.

When the Four Keepers made the world, it took time for it to look like Creator's vision.

Earth was a **tortoise** surrounded by water. In the very center of her back grew one tall tree. One day a sprout appeared next to it. The sprout grew rapidly into another tree. It turned into the first human, a male. This man lived by himself until the tree was tall enough to bend completely over. Where the top of the tree buried itself into the dirt, another sprout appeared. Like the first sprout, this one grew rapidly and became the first woman. This first man and woman were the parents of all people.

Like Creator, people can dream and have visions. They can create and describe their ideas with words. They learn to use words and thoughts carefully so the best world can come into existence.

Delawares, also known as Lenape people, were among the first North Americans to encounter Europeans in New York and New Jersey. Those who lived along the ocean fished and gathered oysters and other shellfish. They drilled beads from shells and used pearls to make beautiful jewelry and robes. They also hunted deer and other game in the forest, like their relatives inland. Many words from the Delaware language entered the English language, like *moccasin, moose*, and *powwow*. The Delawares traded with Europeans, fought, and finally retreated west as more Europeans arrived in the Northeast. Some remain in New Jersey and other places where Delawares have lived. Three Delaware nations are in Oklahoma and Wisconsin. Three more Delaware nations are in Canada. Approximately 15,000 Delawares are enrolled in federally recognized nations.

GLOSSARY

adobe: A type of cement made from clay mixed with straw and often formed into bricks

birch: A tree with white bark that grows in colder climates. Native Americans cut sheets of bark from birch trees for boxes and also for boats and lodges.

briar: Any bushy plant with thorns, like blackberries

canoe: A light, narrow boat with pointed ends. One or more passengers paddle a canoe with an oar. Native Americans used sheets of birchbark to make canoes, especially in the Northeast and around the Great Lakes. In the Pacific Northwest, Native Americans carved dugout canoes from cedar logs.

cedar: An evergreen tree in the United States with soft, fragrant wood and shaggy bark. It has natural oils that make it water resistant. Strands of its inner bark can be woven into mats.

clan: A large group of related people. In Native American communities, a clan may have a specific name, like Towering House or Bear.

copper: A shiny yellow metal. Pennies are made from copper. For thousands of years, Native Americans used copper for tools and ornaments. Copper and gold were the most common metals in the Americas.

council: A meeting of leaders who decide rules for a group of people. Many Native American groups have councils of experienced older people to discuss problems and make decisions.

drought: A period of dry weather without enough rain for plants or animals

eerie: Strange and frightening

elder: An older person. In Native American groups, people respect elders for their years of experience. In some Native American communities, elders hold ceremonial and educational roles.

fast or **fasting:** A time of not eating any food

Kesoq: Menominee word for Sun of the day sky or Moon of the night sky

lodge: A shelter of wood, bark, or animal hides

moccasin: A shoe sewn in one piece without a separate sole. Native Americans invented the moccasin, the name of which comes from the Algonquin language family.

mukluk: A tall snow boot made of fur-lined leather. Arctic Indigenous people, including the Inuit, Inupiat, and Yupik people, wore mukluks in the winter season.

mutton: Meat of a one-year-old sheep that is tougher than lamb. Southwestern Native Americans make stews from mutton.

potlach: A big feast where the host family gives away blankets, food, and other gifts

prairie: A grassland. It may be small or a large region like the tall-grass prairies or Great Plains.

prayer stick: A carved piece of wood of about seven inches long used by Pueblo people to send prayers to spirits. It may be painted or have feathers attached.

silversmith: A person who makes objects from silver

teepee: A cone-shaped shelter made of poles and covered with skins or canvas

tobacco: An herb grown and used by Native Americans for prayers. Tobacco smoke carries prayers to the Creator. Europeans later developed cigarettes and cigars to smoke.

tortoise: A turtle that lives on land

trickster: A person or animal in a story who disobeys rules. A trickster can be playful or greedy. Rabbit and Raven are sometimes trickster figures in Native American stories.

turquoise: A blue-green stone found in the American Southwest used for jewelry and ornaments. China and Iran are also sources of turquoise stones.

vain: To have too high an opinion of oneself. Confidence in oneself is a good thing, but vanity, being vain, is too much confidence.

vision: A sight that is beyond what the eyes can see. A vision in a dream or waking state can tell something about the future.

zigzag: A jagged line made up of angles

MORE TO LEARN

Athabascan

Athabascan people live in the most northern states of the United States. Five major Native groups in Alaska are Southwest Coastal Indians, Inupiats, Yupiks, Aleuts, and Athabascans.

✗ Follow links to all five Native groups in Alaska at Alaska.gov/kids/learn/nativeculture.htm.

✗ Listen to a retelling of the Denali story at NPS.gov/dena /learn/historyculture/legend-of-denali.htm.

Cherokee

Cherokee people continue to tell stories about the trickster rabbit. Sly or greedy people might be today's tricksters. Do you know anyone who has trouble following rules?

✗ Kim Shuck, former San Francisco Poet Laureate and enrolled Cherokee, shares her stories of Rabbit in *Rabbit Stories* (Poetic Matrix Press, 2013).

✗ Gayle Ross, a Cherokee storyteller, reads more stories at YouTube.com/watch?v=VbRzt73Tbdg.

Cheyenne

Today, buffalo, or bison, provide meat for the Cheyenne and other tribal nations. Sweet Medicine's gift of buffalo continues to provide low-fat and high-protein food for everyone.

✗ Find out more about American bison at Kids .NationalGeographic.com/animals/mammals/facts /american-bison.

✗ Read "The Life and Death of Sweet Medicine," as told by members of the Strange Owl family on the Lame Deer Indian Reservation, at AAANativeArts.com /the-life-and-death-of-sweet-medicine.

Delaware (Lenape)

When Europeans arrived in the 1600s, Delaware people borrowed cloth, ribbons, beads, and silver to make their own distinctive dress. They kept deer hide and other native dress—plus their own style.

✗ Explore the online Nanticoke and Lenape Confederation Learning Center and Museum to learn more about Delaware (Lenape) history and culture at NanticokeLenapeMuseum.org.

✗ Read more Delaware stories at DelawareTribe.org /blog/2013/06/27/lenape-stories.

Haida

Haida people used cedar trees for baskets, clothes, and hats. They also carved them into tall totem poles with clan animal designs.

✗ Learn about the craft and meaning of Haida totem poles at YouTube.com/watch?v=MglLs53MX4g.

✗ Learn another view of the Raven at YouTube.com /watch?v=oxA1W7XiteY.

Lakota

Lakotas have great heroes like Crazy Horse, Sitting Bull, and Red Cloud. They represent the courage and intelligence of the Lakota fighting people. Many Lakotas are in the military today.

✗ Visit the Crazy Horse Memorial and its affiliated museums, The Indian Museum of North America and The Native American Educational and Cultural Center, in South Dakota. If you can't go in person, explore the website at CrazyHorseMemorial.org/visit.

✗ Learn more about Lakota culture and read more traditional stories at AktaLakota.STJO.org.

Menominee

This tribal nation named after wild rice, *manomin,* learned to find many kinds of food in their forest homeland.

✕ Explore more Menominee stories passed down by oral tradition at MPM.edu/educators/wirp/nations/menominee/oral-tradition.

✕ Menominee creation accounts vary from clan to clan. Listen to versions in both English and the Menominee language at www4.UWSP.edu/museum/menomineeclans/origin.

Miwok (Southern Sierra)

Miwok tribal members in California value stories as a way to keep their traditions, including respect for land and respect for one another. Stories help prepare children for adulthood.

✕ Read Coast Miwok and Pomo tribal chairman Greg Sarris's book of stories about his homeland, *How a Mountain Was Made: Stories* (Heyday, 2017). Watch him talk about his people at BayBookFest.org/session/timeless-wisdom-greg-sarris-on-telling-tales-and-native-american-literary-tradition (start at 17:00).

✕ Learn more about the Miwok People at Parks.ca.gov/?page_id=22538.

Navajo (Diné)

Half the Navajo clan names refer to towns or places on the reservation, so clan names are also geography lessons. Many other clan names refer to groups that married Navajos, like Naakaii (Mexican).

✗ Learn about clan origin names and marriage partners at TwinRocks.com/legends/general-life-men-women /navajo-clans.html.

✗ Read the creation story of Navajo people at Sacred-Texts .com/nam/nav/ncm/ncm0.htm.

Nez Percé (Nimíipuu)

Land is sacred to most tribal nations, including the Nez Percé, partly because of the sacred stories set in their land. Their creation account is located near present-day Kamiah, Idaho, in a place called Heart of the Monster.

✗ Learn how Yellow Jacket, Coyote, and others made their mark on the geography of Nez Percé country at NPS.gov /nepe/learn/historyculture/nez-perce-stories.htm.

✗ View historic Nez Percé artifacts in the Nez Percé Tribe Wetxuuwíitin Collection at NPS.gov/museum/exhibits /nez_perce_renaming/index.html.

Paiute

People in this tribal nation live in some of the most barren lands, Nevada and surrounding areas, yet they are able to find food sources. Pine nuts are one of the staple foods.

✗ See artifacts from the Paiute and other California and Great Basin nations and tribes at AmericanIndian.SI.edu /exhibitions/infinityofnations/california-greatbasin.html.

✗ Find stories of the Paiutes at FirstPeople.us/FP-Html -Legends/WhytheNorthStarStandsStill-Paiute.html.

Zuni Pueblo (A:shiwi)

Every year, a group of Zuni elders raft down the Colorado River through the Grand Canyon to see sacred sites and petroglyphs. They offer prayers to their ancestors along the way.

✗ See a video of Zuni elders traveling by raft on the Colorado River to the places where their ancestors emerged from the earth at YouTube.com/watch?v =wMSLgYb3M8Y.

✗ Watch and listen to Pueblo stories, including Zuni stories, at IndianPueblo.org/stories.

REFERENCES

Athabascan

Demientieff, Mitch. "The Legend of Denali." 2016. National Park Service: Denali Park and Preserve. NPS.gov/dena/learn/historyculture/legend-of -denali.htm.

Cherokee

Mooney, James. "The Rabbit and the Tar Wolf." *Myths of the Cherokee,* Government Printing Office, 1902. Sacred-Texts.com/nam/cher/motc/motc021.htm.

Cheyenne

"The Life and Death of Sweet Medicine." Told by members of the Strange Owl family on the Lame Deer Indian Reservation, Montana, 1967. AAANativeArts.com/the -life-and-death-of-sweet-medicine.

Delaware (Lenape)

Red Hawk, Robert. "The Lenape Creation Story." Compiled by Zack Wiener. MOAM.info/stories-in-the-lenape -language_59c427391723ddcff423fba4.html.

Haida

"Salmon Boy." FirstPeople.us/FP-Html-Legends
/SalmonBoy-Haida.html.

Lakota

"The Legend of the Flute." Akta Lakota Museum and
Cultural Center. AktaLakota.StJo.org/site/News2?page
=NewsArticle&id=8821.

Menominee

Weso, Thomas Pecore. "Kesoq the Sun Melts the Ice."
Traditional Menominee narrative account.

Miwok (Southern Sierra)

"A Young Hero Fights a Grizzly Bear: The Origin of
Yosemite." FirstPeople.us/FP-Html-Legends
/TheOriginOfYosemite-Miwok.html.

Navajo (Diné)

Klah, Hasteen. *Navajo Creation Myth: The Story of the
Emergence.* Recorded by Mary C. Wheelwright. Navajo
Religion Series, 1942. Sacred-Texts.com/nam/nav/ncm
/ncm0.htm.

Nez Percé (Nimíipuu)

"How the Beaver Stole Fire from the Pines." FirstPeople.us
/FP-Html-Legends/HowTheBeaverStoleFireFromThe
Pines-NezPerce.html.

Paiute

"Why the North Star Stands Still." Traditional story. FirstPeople.us/FP-Html-Legends/WhytheNorthStar StandsStill-Paiute.html.

Zuni Pueblo (A:shiwi)

Cushing, Frank H. "Creation and the Origin of Corn." Originally published as *Zuni Breadstuff*. 1884. Sacred-Texts.com/nam/zuni/cushing/cush07.htm.

ABOUT THE AUTHOR

Thomas Pecore Weso learned stories from his elders on the Menominee reservation in Wisconsin. He makes presentations throughout the country and on Zoom. He is the author of *Good Seeds: A Menominee Indian Food Memoir* (Wisconsin Historical Society Press, 2016). Weso earned his master's degree from the University of Kansas. He now lives in northern California. Visit his website at TomWeso.com.

ABOUT THE ILLUSTRATOR

Gloria Félix is a Púrepecha artist born and raised in Uruapan, a beautiful small city in Michoacán, Mexico. Her hometown and culture are some of her biggest inspirations when it comes to art. After studying 3D animation, Félix moved to San Francisco to get an MFA in Visual Development. In addition to illustrating children's books, she makes art for the animation industry. Her hobbies include walking, life drawing, and plein air painting with her partner and friends. Currently she lives and paints in Guadalajara.